T5-BQA-920

010

NOPL @ Brewerton
5437 Library Street
Brewerton, NY 13029

ON THE TRAIL OF HENRY HUDSON ~ AND OUR ~ DUTCH HERITAGE

THROUGH THE MUNICIPAL SEALS IN NEW YORK...

1609 to 2009

Compiled by Marvin W. Bubie

On the Trail of Henry Hudson and Our Dutch Heritage:
Throught the Municipal Seals of New York.

Copyright © 2009 by Marvin Bubie

All rights reserved. No part of this book may be used or reproduced in any manner whatsoever without written permission from the author except in the case of brief quotation embodied in critical articles and reviews.

To order additional copies of this title,
contact your favorite local bookstore or visit www.tbmbooks.com

Printed in the United States of America

The image used for the seal on the cover is a Thread Painted Quilt, created by Barbara Brown for the Town of Stuyvesant for the Quadricentennial.

The Troy Book Makers
www.thetroybookmakers.com

ISBN: 978-1-935534-0-82

*This book is dedicated to Florence (Bubie) Hill,
former Historian for the Town of Poestenkill for 56
years. Her passion for the past inspired my interest
in history, genealogy and in writing. She was the
author of several books about her hometown.*

Disclaimer

This book is a result of a project that got out of hand. Growing up in the Albany-Troy-Schenectady area, I have always known something about our unique Dutch heritage. When researching the various County, City, Town and village seals, I found more than I expected. While I have tried to include are those municipalities that have a Dutch name, or that have some Dutch symbolism in their seal, or those communities that were founded by the Dutch, I may have missed some. Some communities along the Hudson River claim other than a Dutch heritage by the history as found on their websites. Others have had significant Revolutionary War events depicted on their seals. Some depict the industrial or agricultural themes. If there was still a significant Dutch heritage, I chose to be inclusive. Cohoes, Peekskill, Poughkeepsie all have seals that do not illustrate any Dutch symbols, but were settled by the Dutch.

The inclusion of any municipal seal does not imply endorsement of this book in any way. In addition, many of the seals included are protected by copyright and permission is required prior to their use.

FOREWORD

The Hudson River Valley has an uncommon heritage in New York and even in the rest of the country. In addition to the usual background from the larger European countries, we also have a unique Dutch heritage.

Our Dutch heritage is expressed in many ways including the names of our municipalities, universities, and the people listed in the phone books.

Another way is in the official municipal seals – our elected government leaders conduct official business and press conferences from behind podiums with official seals on them. Larger versions can be found in the Council Chambers or Judicial Chambers, where legal decisions are made. Seals are also on the official government letterheads, web sites, and even on our police and fire vehicles.

We celebrate the Tulip Festival annually, and we award the "Dutchman's Shoes" trophy to the winner of the annual football game between Rensselaer Polytechnic Institute and Union College.

The seals reflect the pride and connection we feel to our heritage. We get to choose them through our Board of Supervisors or Town Councils. So in this area of New York, you will find windmills, and illustrations of a 17th century sailing ship and in unique Dutch names – Rensselaer, Watervliet, Stuyvesant, Patroon, Van Dyck, Schuyler, Van Curler, etc.

These illustrations are found on everyday correspondence and on the streets of our communities. 400 years after Henry Hudson and 345 years after the Dutch formally relinquished claim to NY, the Dutch influence is both subtle and pervasive. The illustrations are a part of our daily lives.

Marvin Bubie
2009

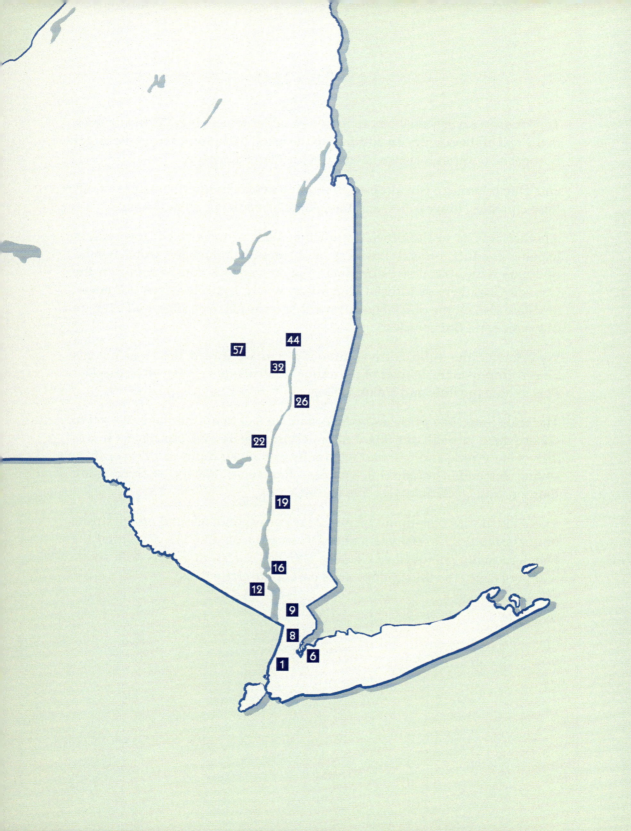

Contents

NEW YORK CITY

New York City has one of the oldest seals having adopted it in 1686. It contains an illustration of the beaver similar to the seal of New Amsterdam.

Also pictured is a sailor representing the Dutch on the Dexter side and a Brave who represents the Lenni Lenape on the Sinister. The eagle on the crest replaced the crown in 1783. New York County (Manhattan) has a similar seal. The Latin is translated simply as The Seal of New York City.

This City of New York Seal is used with the permission from the City of New York.

CONTINUED ON PAGE 60

STATEN ISLAND

In 1609 Henry Hudson names the island Staaten Eyelandt in honor of the Dutch Parliament – the States General or Staaten. Over the next 60 years the Dutch leave a lasting legacy through many Dutch named places and geographical features.

Within the seal appears the color blue to symbolize the skyline of the borough in which two seagulls appear colored in white. The green outline represents the countryside of our borough with white outline denoting the residential areas of Staten Island. Below is inscribed the words STATEN ISLAND in gold. The five wavy lines of blue symbolize the water surrounding us on all sides.

Staten Island became a Borough in 1977, when the Former Borough of Richmond changed its name.

BOROUGH OF BROOKLYN

Within the seal appears a figure of the goddess of justice in gold holding Roman fasces in her left hand set on a background of light blue.

Encircling her figure on a background of dark blue appear the words "Een Draght Mackt Maght" the old Dutch motto for "In unity there is strength" and below the words "borough of Brooklyn." The outside and inside trim of the seal is gold.

BOROUGH OF QUEENS

Two flowers, the tulip and the rose, are surrounded by a circle of wampum, which is taken from the Indian name for Long Island, "Seawanhaka," or "island of sea shells." The first settlers are represented by the two flowers: the tulip, emblematic of the Dutch and the double red and white rose of the English, representing the Houses of York and Lancaster. The Queen's Crown signifies the name of the County and Borough in honor of Queen Catherine of Braganza, wife of Charles II, King of England. The date indicates the year in which Queens County became a part of the City of New York on January 1, 1898.

NE CEDE MALIS

THE BRONX

The Bronx Flag contains the same three horizontal stripes as the colonial Dutch flag. The flag and use of the coat of arms was designed in 1912.

In the center, and extending into the orange stripe above and the blue stripe below, there is the Bronck family crest encircled by a laurel wreath.

In 1748, the oldest house in the Bronx is built by Frederick Van Cortlandt.

NASSAU COUNTY

"The first resolution of the Nassau County Board of Supervisors on Jan 3, 1899 was for a County Coat of Arms, Seal and Flag and to use the same design used by the House of Nassau, Netherlands."

The coat of arms was to include, "Arms, azure, lion rampant or between seven billets."

-Nassau website

TOWN OF OYSTER BAY

"On June 4th, I anchored in a commodious haven on the north of Long Island. We found fine oysters there, from which the Dutch call it Oyster Bay."

- Diary of David deVries, Voyager, 1639.

Sagamore Hill in Oyster Bay was the home of Theodore Roosevelt (of Dutch heritage) from 1886 until his death in 1919.

The seal features a seagull on an yellow background.

– from town website

CITY OF YONKERS

In the late 1640's (about 20 years after Peter Minuit bought Manhattan Island), Adriaen Van der Donck received a grant of land from the Dutch East India Company which he called Colon Donck ("Donck's Colony"), and built one of the first saw mills in the New World at the junction of the Hudson and Nepperhan Rivers. Van der Donck was referred to as Jonk Herr ("young Gentleman" or "young Nobleman") by reason of his status in Holland, and these words evolved through several changes to the Jonk Heer's land and The Younckers, The Yonkers and finally to the present Yonkers. The city was incorporated in 1872.

The seal is a bust of George Washington.

VILLAGE OF TARRYTOWN
(WESTCHESTER COUNTY)

The first settlers were Dutch. The area was suitable for growing wheat and it was called Terve Town which was mispronounced as Tarrytown.

The seal depicts the capture of Major John Andre, by John Paulding, David Williams and Isaac Van wart, all citizens of Tarrytown. This event prevented Benedict Arnold from succeeding in his plan to capture West Point and possibly losing the Revolutionary War.

VILLAGE OF SLEEPY HOLLOW

In 1655 Adriaen Van der Donck, a Dutch colonist, first published a work which referred to the Pocantico River as Slapershaven or, literally, Sleepers' Haven. Sleepy Hollow appears to be a later, Anglicized version of this name and actually applied to the valley of the Pocantico River. It now serves as the name of the incorporated village.

In the late 1790s Washington Irving came to visit his friend and relative, James K. Paulding, in Tarrytown. Together the two young men explored the area of Sleepy Hollow, hunting and fishing and talking with local folk. The fruits of Irving's visits were later to be immortalized in the story "The Legend of Sleepy Hollow." In it the father of American literature drew heavily from Sleepy Hollow's landscape and customs.

by Henry Steiner-Village of Sleepy Hollow Historian

ROCKLAND COUNTY

Some of the earliest Dutch settlers — eager to escape "city life" in the New Amsterdam colony — moved to Rockland (then part of Orange County) in the early 1600s. During the first half of the century, they cleared the land, built homes, schools and churches. They have historic farms — many in the same family since the 1600s. The 1700 DeWint House is our oldest standing residence.

TOWN OF HAVERSTRAW
(ROCKLAND COUNTY)

In 1609 Henry Hudson sailed his ship as far as what is now Albany and on the return trip the Half Moon anchored in what is now Haverstraw Bay, the widest point in the river. Haverstraw is one of the oldest names in the geography of North America. The word is Dutch and it first appeared on a map in 1616. It was originally written "Haverstroo" and means oat straw, descriptive of the waving straw of the river meadows.

ORANGE COUNTY

Orange County was established in 1683 as one of the original counties of the Province of New York. The county name is derived primarily after Prince William III of the Netherlands House of Orange. After the death of England's Queen Mary, he reigned as William III of England. The name was meant to honor both England and the Netherlands.

The seal has been in use at least since the late 1700's.

DUTCHESS COUNTY

One of the original counties formed in Colonial New York in 1683, the County Seal is also one of the oldest, seen in very old records.

From 1683-1725 most of the settlers in Dutchess County were Dutch. Many of these moved in from Albany and Ulster Counties.

The Great Seal is representative of a plow and stems of ripened wheat.

Many early seals had agricultural themes.

TOWN OF FISHKILL
(DUTCHESS COUNTY)

In 1683, nineteen years after the Dutch surrendered New Amsterdam to the English, Frances Rombout and Gulian Verplanck, purchased 85,000 acres in Dutchess County from the Wappinger Indians. Their house, built about 1709, still stands in Beacon, and is the oldest continuous residence in Dutchess County. The name Fishkill is derived from two Dutch words: Vis (fish) and Kill (creek or stream).

Willa Skinner, Town Historian

CITY OF PEEKSKILL
(WESTCHESTER COUNTY)

The Peekskill region was first identified by European immigrants as "Peeck's Kill." This name was adapted from the explorer and fur businessman Jan Peeck. Thus, Mr. Peeck, or Peak, or Peek (according to various spellings), and the Dutch word for stream or creek, (which is "kill" or "kil") were combined as this place name. The area was known to the Dutch as "Jan Peeck's kill," and to the English as "John Peak's Creek." In 1685 the written deed transfer of land for these items was the Ryck's Patent. The seal depicts the industry that came later in history.

TOWN OF HYDE PARK

Hyde Park was originally settled by Jacobus Stoutenburg, of Dutch descent, in 1742 and was known at that time by the family name. He was a descendant of Peter van Stoutenburg of Amersfoot, Pays d'Utrecht, Netherlands. His most notable position was the first Treasurer of New Amsterdam (New York City). The town was officially named Hyde Park in 1812.

The Seal of Hyde Park is variation of the Stoutenburg family crest with three roses to represent the Roosevelt family. Roosevelt means "field of roses" in Dutch. Franklin Roosevelt's ancestors were of Dutch lineage and he was godfather to Princess Margriet of the Netherlands born in 1943.

The Town of Hyde Park uses the silhouette of FDR's bust as their logo.

TOWN OF RHINEBECK
(DUTCHESS COUNTY)

"The Rhinebeck town Seal provides a history lesson of the Town. The upper left represents the British flag and the lower right represents the Dutch flag. Settlers from both nations were early founders. The water wheel symbolizes the importance of water as an energy source to early Rhinebeck. The lower left contains violets, commemorating Rhinebeck industry. The overlay in the middle pays homage to Palatine settlers of 1710."

-Nancy Kelly, Town Historian

SEAL OF THE CITY OF POUGHKEEPSIE

1799

INCORPORATED 1854

CITY OF POUGHKEEPSIE
(DUTCHESS COUNTY)

The first settlers were Dutch, and among the first, if not the first, was Baltus VAN KLEECK. Founded in 1687, the community became an incorporated village in 1799, and the city was chartered in 1854. Poughkeepsie was the state capital of New York from 1777 through 1783. In 1788, New York State ratified the United States Constitution at the Market Street courthouse. The beehive as a city symbol is one of the oldest in the world dating back to biblical times.

ULSTER COUNTY

Ulster County is one of the original counties established in Colonial New York in 1683. The current seal is a variation of the original that dates back to the colonial period as well.

The seal of the county represents the Catskill Mountains, a sheaf of grain, a pre-revolutionary farmer and a Dutch stone house".

CITY OF KINGSTON
(ULSTER COUNTY)

In 1609, the Half Moon passed by the creek near which the future Kingston would be built. Some historians believe that, by 1614, a small trading post had been established on the Hudson near present-day Kingston. In 1652, a handful of settlers from Holland moved down from near Albany. In 1653, they arranged to purchase land from the Esopus, a tribe of the Delaware Nation, and to farm near them. On the slight promontory overlooking the flood plains, they built houses in a village that they first called Esopus, and later Wiltwyck (Dutch for "wild woods"). The famous Hudson River Sloop (Dutch Sloop) reminds us of the commercial and travel purposes of the River.

CONTINUED ON PAGE 60

VILLAGE OF SAUGERTIES
(ULSTER COUNTY)

The northern boundary was roughly identified with a stream called the Sawyer's Kill, where a Dutchman named Barent Cornelis Volge operated a sawmill in the 1650s for the manor of Rensselaerswick.

The name Saugerties means "Little Sawyer" in Dutch, apparently a reference to Volge.

The seal illustrates a mill with the water wheel for power.

GREENE COUNTY

The Dutch were the first European settlers, arriving in the early part of the 17th century. Development took place along the Hudson River where the Dutch built several farmsteads. Today these early Dutch homes are historic and scenic attractions. The Bronck House is an excellent example and serves as the home of the Greene County Historical Society.

Depicted on the seal are the Hudson River and the Catskill Mountains.

VILLAGE OF CATSKILL
(GREENE COUNTY)

Rip Van Winkle is an American story of a Dutch settler who sleeps for 20 years and dreams of watching Henry Hudson and his crew playing 9-pins in the Catskill Mountains.

The Half Moon is illustrated in Rip Van Winkle's beard.

COLUMBIA COUNTY

Henry Hudson's ship is depicted in the background, along with the figure of Columbia holding a law book, and a stage coach. The establishments of Fort Orange and New Amsterdam in 1624 allowed traders and travelers to frequently stop along the shores of Columbia.

The county was formed in 1786.

CITY OF HUDSON
(COLUMBIA COUNTY)

The City of Hudson is the only municipality in New York named in honor of Henry Hudson. The Dutch arrived in the 17th Century. One of them, Franz VanHoesen purchased a large tract of land from the Indians. His farm included the area of Hudson, plus part of what is now Greenport. Originally called Claverack Landing, it was renamed in 1785 as the City of Hudson and was the third city in the state. In the late 1700's and early 1800's Hudson was the home of a thriving whaling industry. The seal was adopted by the Common Council in 1998.

TOWN OF CLAVARACK
(COLUMBIA COUNTY)

According to one version, the name "CLAVERACK" is a Dutch term signifying a clover reach or field...applied by Henry Hudson during his voyage up river in 1609 when the explorer noted vast fields of white clover covering the landscape. Claverack became a town on March 7, 1788.

The seal was adopted on December 10, 1984 and was designed by Florence Mossman.

CONTINUED ON PAGE 61

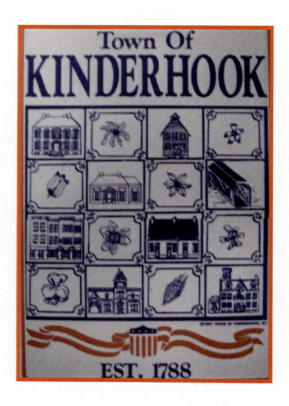

TOWN OF KINDERHOOK
(COLUMBIA COUNTY)

Kinderhook was named by Henry Hudson in 1609 when he saw Indian children playing and called it kinder hook or "children's corner."

The town logo or seal represents Dutch Delft tiles and depict various historic buildings in the town including early Dutch homes and Lindenwald, the home of Martin Van Buren, 8th President of the US. One of the flowers illustrated is a tulip.

CONTINUED ON PAGE 62

VILLAGE OF VALATIE
(COLUMBIA COUNTY)

Valatie, whose name in Dutch was Vaaltje, means "Little Falls", is named after two waterfalls, from the Kinderhook Creek and the Valatie Kill.

The Dutch came to the junction of the Kinderhook and Valatie kills about 1650, trappers and hunters in search of furs, particularly beaver.

The seal honors the Beaver Cotton Mill (destroyed in 1888) that was significant in the history of the village.

TOWN OF STUYVESANT
(COLUMBIA COUNTY)

400 years ago, as the intrepid Henry Hudson made his way up the river that now bears his name, he happened upon an area of pristine beauty and economic promise. Investigating further, Hudson - always a good judge of character - determined that the natives were friendly and welcoming. He immediately dropped anchor and made landfall in what would later become Stuyvesant, New York.

The logo depicts the Half Moon and the town carries a Dutch name. from Town of Stuyvesant website

ALBANY COUNTY

At the center of the seal is a silhouette of the *Half Moon* which references Henry Hudson's historic 1609 voyage and the Dutch character of the early settlement. The ship is surrounded by winterberry, a local plant which represents the county's natural heritage. The county's incorporation date is 1683 and is one of the original counites of colonial New York. John Merril was the designer of the new seal which was approved in 1995 by the State Legislature and then Gov. George Pataki. Albany County Clerk Thomas Clingan was instrumental in the process of adopting a more appropraite seal than the earlier one which did not reference the founding date.

CITY OF ALBANY
(FORMERLY FORT ORANGE)

It was on July 22, 1686 that Governor Thomas Dongan representing the British crown granted a charter recognizing Albany as a city. Dongan also appointed Pieter Schuyler as the first mayor. Since that time 74 men have served as mayor of which 34 had Dutch heritage.

Originally Fort Orange under the Dutch, when the English took control it was renamed "Albany," in honor of the Duke of York and Albany, who later became James VII of Scotland and II of England. The Duke of Albany is a Scottish title given since 1398, generally to a younger son od a Scottish King. The name is derived from Alba; the Gaelic name for Scotland.

CONTINUED ON PAGE 64

TOWN OF NEW SCOTLAND
(ALBANY COUNTY)

The windmill reflects our Dutch heritage, the thistle symbolizes our Scottish background, the mountains and ladder denote the Helderbergs and the Indians who lived there, with a fire bush for Feuera Bush also included.

The seal was drawn by Timothy Albright in 1975 as a result of a contest sponsored by the Daughters of the American Revolution and the New Scotland Historical Society.

-From Town of New Scotland

TOWN OF BETHLEHEM
(ALBANY COUNTY)

The Indian represents a Mohawk Indian and symbolizes the treaty to commemorate the beaver trade with the Dutch in 1617. The figure of Henry Hudson and an illustration of his ship, the Half Moon commemorate his arrival in 1609.

After Henry Hudson's journey in 1609, early settlement of the Town of Bethlehem began along the Hudson. In 1649 the name Bethlehem referred to the settlement at the confluence of the Hudson and Vloman's Kill.

The seal was drawn by Alice Pauline Shafer and adopted by the Bethlehem Town Board in 1975.

CITY OF WATERVLIET
(ALBANY COUNTY)

Watervliet means "flowing water" in Dutch.

The seal contains illustrations of the rising sun over the hills east of the Hudson, a sheaf of wheat and a cornucopia, to signify the bounty of the land, the Clermont, and a Dutch sloop. The seal had its origins around the time the city was incorporated in 1896.

GUILDERLAND BICENTENNIAL

1803 2003

TWO HUNDRED YEARS OF PRIDE

PROSPICE GELRIA

TOWN OF GUILDERLAND
(ALBANY COUNTY)

The coat of arms was adopted from the coat of arms of the Province of Gelderland, Holland by permission granted by a letter dated March 11, 1959 signed by the Queens's Commissioner. English translation of the motto on riband is "look forward Guilderland".

TOWN OF COLONIE
(ALBANY COUNTY)

"The Town Seal was officially adopted on May 8, 1941, and symbolizes the origin and background of the town. In the upper left hand quarter of the seal is the Indian head which represents the first inhabitants, whose arrowheads are still found in the surrounding fields. In the upper right the sheaf of wheat indicates the predominant occupation of the townspeople at the time the town was founded in 1895. Below the Indian head is the fort which relates to the name of the town, Colonie, meaning in Dutch, 'the settlement outside the city.' In the lower right quarter stands the windmill signifying the Dutch heritage of the town's permanent settlers. Surrounding the four quarters is the wampum circle which represents the important trade routes that pass through and border the town. The spray of laurel and sheaf of wheat signify a future of success and plenty."

–Historian of Colonie

CONTINUED ON PAGE 65

CITY OF COHOES
(ALBANY COUNTY)

The City of Cohoes, located at the junction of the Mohawk and Hudson Rivers, was developed on land bought from the Indians in 1630 by Kiliaen Van Rensselaer, a director of the Dutch West India Company. Up to the time of the revolution, Cohoes was strictly an agricultural area. The seal represents a time later in the City's history as an industrial center.

TOWN OF RENSSELAERVILLE
(ALBANY COUNTY)

The Dutch patroons Van Rensselaer and part of the huge Manor of Rensselaerwyck owned the area now known as Rensselaerville. It was formed on March 8, 1790. Settlement did not take place until the late 1700's. Mills were very important to farmers and settlers. The Grist Mill pictured here was built in 1880 to replace previous mills on the site that burned.

The town celebrates the mill that still exists.

SCHENECTADY COUNTY

When Dutch settlers arrived in the Hudson Valley in the middle of the 17th century, the Mohawk called the settlement at Fort Orange "Schau-naugh-ta-da," meaning "over the pine plains." Eventually, this word entered the lexicon of the Dutch settlers, but the meaning was reversed, and the name referred to the bend in the Mohawk River where the city lies today.

Arent Van Curler along with fourteen other landholders settled along the Mohawk in 1661 on a piece of land that eventually became the city of Schenectady. In 1765, Schenectady was incorporated as a borough. It was chartered as a city in 1798.

The scales of justice beneath the crossed swords, represents strength and justice. The colors (blue and orange) are borrowed from the colonial Dutch flag.

CITY OF SCHENECTADY

The City Seal was engraved in 1800 at a cost of $11.00 as described by the Schenectady Historical Society. The shock of wheat recalls the "fair land" of the Mohawk Valley and symbolizing peace and plenty.

Eighty-five years before Paul Revere's ride, on February 8th 1690, the French and their Indian allies attacked the Dutch Village of Schenectady and massaccred sixty inhabitants. Although wounded, Symon Schermerhorn rode twenty miles to warn the citizens of Albany. His ride is re-enacted each year.

VILLAGE OF SCOTIA
(SCHENECTADY COUNTY)

In the 1650's, Alexander Lindsey of Glen bought land along the river from the Iroquois Indians. While he emigrated to the new world with Dutch settlers, he named his estate Scotia, in memory of his native Scottish hills. The Glen Sanders mansion illustrated here is described as having – "A large Dutch cleft door opens into a hallway…" "The house is English in style, though the wing or L in rear, has the characteristic sharp Dutch gable."

TOWN OF NISKAYUNA
(SCHENECTADY COUNTY)

The Niskayuna Bicentennial Town Seal was designed by area resident Robert Banks and was adopted in 1976. The upper right side depicts an Indian holding an ear of corn. The five tepees in the background represent the Five Nations. The name NISKAYUNA means "land of extended corn fields." The lower right portrays a Shaker farmer; upper left pictures an Erie Canal boat in tow; and lower left is the atomic symbol, for modern industry in Niskayuna. In the center is a map outline of the town with typical crops below the stonework-styled letter "N".

CONTINUED ON PAGE 65

TOWN OF HALFMOON
(SARATOGA COUNTY)

The only illustration is a ship under full sail representing Henry Hudson's ship and the year that the town was established. This is the logo rather than an official seal but it is used on the Town vehicles, on official Town sites, including parks, etc. There are several variations of this design used on letterhead stationery, the Town Flag, and designs surrounding the entrances to the Town buildings.

TOWN OF CLIFTON PARK

(SARATOGA COUNTY)

...at the top of the shield are two flag which represent the two European nations which had a great deal of importance to the development of the Town of Clifton Park. On the dexter side is the red-white-blue tricolor of the Netherlands, indicating the salience of the Dutch, while on the sinister side is the Union Jack of the British Isles as it looked prior to the American Revolution.....

SEE FULL TEXT ON PAGE 64

RENSSELAER COUNTY

Rensselaer County was formed in 1791 and is named for the Dutch family of Killiaen Van Rensselaer who owned the land and was the 1st patroon. The official seal is simply an outline of the county and the towns within its borders. The Seal of the Rensselaer County Legislature is much more interesting. There is virtually no information on its significance. There are various symbols – a steam locomotive and a clipper ship would represent the importance of transportation. In the background is a factory representing the importance of manufacturing. In the foreground are tools of agriculture recognizing its importance to Rensselaer County's history. The central figure though is a mystery. After the Revolutionary War, there was a trend of classical names for cities such as Troy, Utica, Syracuse, Rome and Ithaca. Since Troy was named in 1789 and is the county seat, there is a possibility of a figure from Classical literature. (The Troy seal depicts the riverfront prior to any bridges on the river).

CITY OF TROY
(RENSSELAER COUNTY)

One of the earliest settlers was Derick Vanderheyden who obtained title to 490 acres in 1720. No records exist of the origin of the seal, however, the symbols depicted has been used on other seals before 1800 to indicate major trading goods such as barrels of flour, bales of fur, and sheaves of wheat. In the background are illustrations of Dutch sloops used to transport goods on the Hudson River.

CITY OF RENSSELAER
(RENSSELAER COUNTY)

The seal was designed by Ernie Mann and he had three themes. Rensselaer is the home of Yankee Doodle Dandy where an English officer, Dr. Richard Shuckburgh, sat on a well and wrote a derisive tune about the American soldier. The ship is the Half Moon that docked here in 1609. The third theme is transportation symbolized by a steam locomotive built in the area and serviced at the rail yard in Rensselaer.

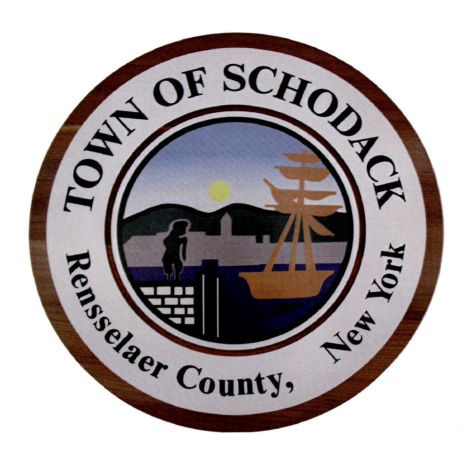

TOWN OF SCHODACK
(RENSSELAER COUNTY)

The history of the development of the seal is not clear. The image depicts a stylized view of Henry Hudson's ship and the Hudson River near Castleton. Sometime before 1986, a contest was held by a Maple Hill School teacher named Connie Dodge. The winner was Ms Mancini. This contest may have been held in conjunction with the Bicentennial in 1976.

TOWN OF STEPHENTOWN
(RENSSELAER COUNTY)

The shield represents the Van Rensselaer Coat-of-Arms and is used with permission of Stephen Van Rensselaer, the Great-great-grandson of our founder Stephan Van Rensselaer III. The wording is arranged in a circle as a symbol of unity. The dividers are peaks depicting the Taconic and Petersburg Ranges. The numbers of peaks denote our three towns, Stephentown, Stephentown Center and West Stephentown.

TOWN OF POESTENKILL
(RENSSELAER COUNTY)

During the 1660s, Jan Barentsen Wemp (also recorded as Jan Barentsen Poest in the early records of the colony) built a lumber mill on the creek now referred to as Poesten kill. The most widely accepted version of the name is that the Dutch "Poest" means rushing, dirty, foamy and "kill" means creek. The town derived its name from the Poestenkill Creek, which flows through it and became a town in 1848.

The logo was designed by Barbara Woldt and chosen by the Town in 1982 as a result of a contest. It illustrates the creek as well as the broad shouldered hills surrounding the town and the churches which have been a part of the town since the early 1800s.

TOWN OF SAND LAKE
(RENSSELAER COUNTY)

The first permanent settlements in Sand Lake were made in its western part, probably in 1765 or 1766. They were sturdy Dutch farmers who had come from Holland a few years after the settlement of Albany, or who had first located further down the Hudson Valley. The first two families were Adams and Brett (or Brandt). The majority of settlers that came later were mostly German and Scotch. Jeremiah Van Rensselaer founded the Rensselaer Glass Works in 1804 on land from Patroon Van Rensselaer.

The logo depicts a large oak tree and the Town Hall (at the time) which was the former Sand Lake Presbyterian Church until 1967. The Town Hall being in a former church reminds us of the central role that religion has always played in the town and the oak tree reminds us of the lumber business that was a part of the town's early history. The logo for the Town of Sand Lake was designed by Patricia Brock and was chosen in May 1985 as a result of a contest.

- Landmarks of Rensselaer County by George Anderson, Sand Lake Historical Society

TOWN OF NORTH GREENBUSH
(RENSSELAER COUNTY)

The town seal was chosen by the Town Board from a contest won by a second grader possibly in conjunction with the country's bicentennial in 1976. The illustration features the Wynantskill Creek which flows through Wynantskill, where the Town Offices are located.

The Wynantskill was named after Wynant Gerritse Van Der Poel, part owner of a mill on the creek as of 1674. North Greenbush was carved out of a parcel of land granted to Patroon Stephen Van Rensselaer and became a town in 1855.

Landmarks of Rensselaer County, 1897

TOWN OF PITTSTOWN
(RENSSELAER COUNTY)

The Town of Pittstown was given its name by King George III in 1761, in honor of the William Pitt, earl of Chatham. The first settlers were of Dutch origin, occupying lands deeded to them by the Van Rensselaer's. Early settlers were mainly farmers, bearing names such as Bleeker, Brant, Clark, Colden, De Peyster, Lansing, Sawyer and Van Cortland to mention a few.

TOWN OF HOOSICK
(RENSSELAER COUNTY)

Early settlers were Dutch. Among the pioneer settlers of the town of Hoosick was Jan Oothout, who prior to 1754 had built a home just inside the present boundaries of the village of Hoosick Falls. Near the junction of the Little Hoosick and Hoosick rivers was a settlement known in colonial times as Hoosack. It lay between Hoosick Corners and North Petersburgh and was partly within the limits of the town of Petersburgh and in the manor of Rensselaerwyck.

WITENAGEMOT OAK
A
MONUMENT
TO PEACE
• 1676 •

SCHAGHTICOKE

TOWN OF SCHAGHTICOKE
(RENSSELAER COUNTY)

The seal depicts the 1676 Witenagemot Council (Assemblage of the Wise) and the Witenagemot Oak. The famous Council Tree of Peace was planted to strengthen the alliance of Fort Albany militia with the River Indian scouts. The white oak of the Schaghticokes lived until it was uprooted by the 1949 flood of the Hoosick River. Also depicted is a plow representing agriculture and a gear representing industry. The first permanent settler of record was Lewis Viele, son of Cornelis Cornelise Viele of Schenectady, who moved to Schaghticoke in 1668. The first grant to lands in Schaghticoke was given to inhabitants of the city of Albany by the charter of 1686. Schaghticoke is the home of the Knickerbocker Family Mansion that dates from 1770 and is on the site of the Witenagemot Oak. The Knickerbocker family has been in Schaghticoke since 1709. The seal was chosen from a contest in 1989.

VILLAGE OF NASSAU
(RENSSELAER COUNTY)

Jonathan Hoag settled in the town in 1792, and became the first Town Supervisor in 1807 when the town was organized under the name of Philipstown in honor of Philip Van Rensselaer. The village was christened "Union Village" in the early 1790's. The Village of Nassau was incorporated on March 12, 1819.

The seal illustrates an elm tree that Nassau was noted for prior to their being destroyed by Dutch Elm disease.

Information courtesy of Margaret Van Deusen, Treasurer

TOWN OF ROTTERDAM
(SCHENECTADY COUNTY)

Rotterdam, New York was first settled predominately by the Dutch, about the year 1661. The town, named after the city of Rotterdam, The Netherlands, was formed from a ward of the city of Schenectady on April 14, 1820. Coat of Arms of the Town of Rotterdam NY granted in 1952 by the Government of the Netherlands.

CITY OF AMSTERDAM
(MONTGOMERY COUNTY)

Amsterdam was named for the city in Holland where many early settlers came from. Originally called Veedersburgh after one of the first settlers named Albert Veeder, Amsterdam was incorporated on April 20, 1830.

The city has a long history of industrialization from the abundant water supply. The seal is an updated version (2009) of the windmill, drawn by **Robert Olbrycht, City businessman.**

NEW YORK CITY
(continued from page 1)

The City Seal:

- *Arms:* Upon a shield, saltire wise, the sails of a windmill. Between the sails, in chief a beaver, in base a beaver, and on each flank a flour barrel.
- *Supporters:* Dexter, a sailor, his right arm bent, and holding in his right hand a plummet; his left arm bent, his left hand resting on the top of the shield; above his right shoulder, a cross-staff. Sinister, an Indian of Manhattan, his right arm bent, his right hand resting on top of the shield, his left hand holding the upper end of a bow, the lower end of which rests on the ground. Shield and supporters rest upon a horizontal laurel branch.
- *Date:* Beneath the horizontal laurel branch the date 1625, being the year of the establishment of New Amsterdam.
- *Crest:* An American eagle with wings displayed, upon a hemisphere.
- *Legend:* Upon a ribbon encircling the lower half of the design the words "Sigillum Civitatis Novi Eboraci," meaning Seal of the City of New York.

The whole is encircled by a laurel wreath.

City of Kingston
(continued from page 21)

Design Specifications:

The official seal of the City of Kingston, New York shall consist of a circular device with the words "City of Kingston, New York" at the top and the date "1652" at the bottom. Also in the outer ring of the circle shall be the traditional olive branch. The pictorial symbols shall consist of: The Senate House, a Hudson River Sloop shown in full sail upon the River, the Catskill Mountains in the background with the Sun rising over the scene.

Design Explanations:

The Senate House represents Kingston's contribution, as first Capitol, to the history of New York State. The Catskill Mountains are a symbol of majesty and permanence. The famous Hudson River Sloop reminds us of the commercial and travel purposes of the River. The Sun with its radial beams brings a constant promise of Kingston's bright future built firmly upon a noble past. The olive branches depict peaceful aspirations. The design as a whole is a significant but not radical departure from the older City Seal. It is emblematical, historical, harmonious.

From the official website of the City of Kingston.

TOWN OF CLAVERACK
"OUR SEAL" (from the Town website)
(continued from page 27)

The seal of the Town of Claverack was adopted by the Claverack Town Board at their meeting on December 10, 1984. This was the first official seal of the town even though it had been legally proclaimed a town on March 7, 1788: when by an act of the State Legislature, the District of Claverack, along with many other New York State Communities became "Towns."

The Seal was designed in 1984 by Florence Mossman, a local resident and the then Historian for the Town of Claverack and the County of Columbia. Ms. Mossman is a graphic artist with 25 years of experience in illustration, writing, and design.

The symbolism in the design of the seal is explained here just as it was to the town meeting on December 10, 1984.

CLOVERS: The clovers were added, not because of the legend of "clover fields" but rather in the folklore tradition, the clover plant symbolizes good soil.

SHEAF OF WHEAT: The sheaf of wheat represents the first settlers who cleared the land and established a farming community.

BELL: The bell has a two-fold meaning ---first it refers to the spiritual life of the early settlers and their desire to establish a place of worship. Secondly, the bell recognizes the settler's desire for education.

MILL WHEEL: The mill wheel symbolizes the grist mills and sawmills that were built along the streams --they were the beginning of industry in the Town.

SCALES and BANNER: With the withdrawal of Columbia County from Albany County in 1786, Claverack became the first seat of county government - the first Courthouse being completed in 1788.

ROPE: The rope signifies the town's tie to the river, when the City of Hudson was known as Claverack Landing.

OFFICIAL SEAL OF THE TOWN OF
KINDERHOOK, NEW YORK
(continued from page 28)

The First Official Seal of the Town of Kinderhook, formally adopted January 13, 1997, is intended to give the appearance of Dutch Delft tile. Dutch tiles usually depict scenes of Dutch life. Authentic tiles imported from one of the many influences the Dutch. Authentic tiles imported from Holland line the fireplaces at the Van Alen Homestead. The tiles symbolize one of the many influences the Dutch settlers had on the Town of Kinderhook.

The tiles in the upper left-handed corner of the design depict the Vanderpoel House. James Vanderpoel who served as Assemblyman, County Surrogate, and was appointed Circuit Judge of the Supreme Court of the State of New York built this house circa 1820. The Columbia County Historical Society purchased the house in 1925.

The third tile in the first row represents a mill. Mills appeared in Valatie as early as 1697. Valatie became one of the earliest industrial centers containing saw mills, grist mills, flour mills, cotton mills, plaster mills and fulling mills. Valatie was at one time nicknamed "Millville". Nathan Wild, a prominent owner of many Valatie mills, started the first power loom that was run in New York State, in one of his mills.

The second tile in the second row represents the Kinderhook Memorial Library, which was built in 1933. The former library was housed in the Masonic Temple where friends donated books. In 1931, Mrs. Caroline Davie Lloyd donated the present site and in 1933, the present building was donated in memory of George Davie.

The fourth tile in the second row represents a covered bridge, Valatie's' covered bridge, which spanned 252 feet across the creek was built in 1792. The Staats Bridge, as it was called, is supposedly the bridge Harry Houdini leaped from in 1924, in making an early silent film "Haldane of the Secret Service".

The first tile in the third row represents the present day Treasure Shop. In 1864 the building was a row of wooden buildings varying in size and architecture. In May of 1880 the entire clock was destroyed by fire. After being "rebuilt", it was purchased in 1882 by the Kinderhook Knitting Company, which added the brick front.

The third tile in the third row depicts the Van Alen homestead. The house was built in 1737 and is a restored example of rural Dutch architecture. Historians believe the bricks were produced locally.

The second tile in the fourth row depicts the First Presbyterian Church, which was built in 1877. Architects Ogden & Wright modeled the church after an old German Cathedral.

The fourth tile in the fourth row depicts Lindenwald, the home of Martin Van

Buren, eighth President of the United States. Peter Van Ness built the house in 1797. Martin Van Buren bought the house in 1841 and added on the tower and a library. The house was deemed Lindenwald for the linden trees, which shelter the house from the road. Martin Van Buren died here in 1862.

The floral tiles depict another side of the Town of Kinderhook. The second tiles in the first and the fourth tile in the third row represent the Black-eyed Susan and the Tiger Lily. These wild flowers brighten country roads and gardens throughout the town in the summer.

The fourth tile in the first row and the first tile in the fourth row represent the Violet and the Pansy. These flowers have developed from European species just as Kinderhook has developed from European influence.

The first tile in the second row and the second tile in the third row represent the Tulip and the Daffodil. These two flowers frequent the gardens of town inhabitants in the spring. The Tulip also stands as a reminder of the Dutch influence on the Town.

The third tile in the second row and the third tile in the fourth row represent an Apple Blossom and a Wheat Shaft. Apple orchards make up a fair share of the town and produce lucrative crops. The wheat shaft represents the town's agricultural background.

In conclusion, Kinderhook is a brilliant Town that can be stately and rustic, conservative and original. This logo is meant to capture the spirit of Kinderhook, its glorious past and promising future.

[HISTORY: Adopted by the Common Council of the City of Albany 7-18-1983 by L.L. No. 2-1983 as Ch. I, Art. I, of the 1983 Code. Amendments noted where applicable.]

GENERAL REFERENCES

Facsimile signature and seal — See Ch. 18.

§ 15-1 Description.

The device of arms of the City of Albany, adopted pursuant to resolutions of the Common Council passed December 16, 1789, and January 9, 1790, is hereby reestablished and readopted and declared to be correctly described as follows:

A. Arms: gules, two (2) garbs in fess; or on a chief argent, at the dexter side a beaver contourne, and on his hind feet, his forepaws resting upon a tree stump, erect, which he is gnawing; the tree, fallen, still attached to the stump, fesswise and contourne, all proper.

B. Crest: on a wreath of six (6) twists argent and gules, a Dutch sloop vert, under sail, all proper, pennant flying gules.

C. Supporters: standing upon an extension of the scroll hereafter described:

(1) Dexter supporter: a farmer proper, habited with a deerskin coat, open and showing a white shirt; homespun trousers, bluish gray, buckled shoes, a gray, broad-brimmed felt hat upon his head; his sinister arm embowed, the hand supporting the shield at the dexter chief point; a sickle proper, point to the dexter, hanging over his dexter forearm which rests upon the hip, to the front.

(2) Sinister supporter: an American Indian, savage proper; girded with a beaver skin; moccasined; a feather gules in his scalp lock; an elongated ornament hanging from the ear, argent; a quiver belt leather, trimmed with beads of wampum, passed over the sinister shoulder, the feathers of the arrows showing above the shoulder from behind; his dexter arm embowed, the elbow resting upon and supporting the shield at the sinister chief point, the forearm contourne; his sinister arm embowed, the forearm palewise holding in the hand, just above the shoulder, the top of a strung bow, the string to the sinister, the bow partly disappearing behind the sinister hip and again emerging, its base resting upon the scroll (hereinafter described) all proper.

D. Motto: on the above-mentioned scroll, argent, below the shield and never across it: "Assiduity" in plain Roman letters, gules.

TOWN OF COLONIE SEAL
(continued from page 37)

The Town Seal, adopted on May 8, 1941, symbolizes the background and origin of the Town.

The upper left-hand corner of the seal is the Indian Head which represents the first inhabitants of the Town.

To the right of the Indian Head is the Sheaf of Wheat indicating the predominant occupation of the townspeople when it was founded in 1895.

In the lower left-hand corner is the fort, which relates to the name of the Town, Colonie, from the Dutch "Colonye" meaning "the Settlement outside the city."

In the lower right corner is the windmill, which displays the Dutch heritage of the Town's first permanent settlers.

Surrounding these areas is the Wampum circle, which represents the trade routes that pass through the Town.

The spray of laurel and leaf represent a future of success and plenty.

THE TOWN OF NISKAYUNA
(continued from page 43)

The Niskayuna Bicentennial Town Seal was designed by area resident Robert Banks who is a Niskayuna resident.

In explanation of its artistry, the upper right side depicts an Indian holding an ear of corn.

The five tepees in the background represent the Five Nations.

The name NISKAYUNA means "land of extended corn fields."

The lower right portrays a Shaker farmer; upper left pictures an Erie Canal boat in tow; and lower left is the atomic symbol, for modern industry in Niskayuna.

In the center of the map is an outline of the town, with typical crops below the stonework-styled letter "N."

The Town was established in 1809 which accounts for the date.

From HISTORY OF NISKAYUNA, NEW YORK edited by Mrs. Margaret Harder and Mrs. Jay Johnson

CLIFTON PARK TOWN SEAL
(continued from page 45)

This seal emphasizes the heritage and history of the Town of Clifton Park and the area which it comprises. It contains several motifs all of which are significant.

The semicircular garland of corn sheaves on the dexter side of the seal represent the agricultural fruition of the area' first known denizens, the Indians. The area along the Mohawk River called "Canastigione" or "corn flats" by these aboriginies and the stylized corn is in tribute to the Indians and their agricultural accomplishments.

The semicircular garland of wheat on the sinister side of the seal is symbolic of the general importance of agriculture in the town's economy during the 19th and 20th centuries. More particularly, it denotes the significance of grain agriculture in this area.

In the middle of the seal is a shield which is divided into here distinct sections:

a) At the top of the shield are two flags which represent the two European nations which had a great deal of importance to the development of the Town of Clifton Park. On the dexter side is the red-white-blue tricolor of the Netherlands, indicating the salience of the Dutch, while on the sinister side is the Union Jack of the British Isles as it looked prior to the American Revolution. This of course represents the town's recognition of its English roots.

b) In the middle of the shield is a constellation of five five-pointed stars arranged in a semicircular pattern above a stylized half-moon. These stars represent the five primary villages which are historically salient in the town's history, especially through the 19th and 20th centuries: Vischer Ferry (Amity), Jonesville (Elnora), Clifton Park (the town's namesake), Grooms Corners, and Rexford Flats. The half-moon represents the recognition of our town's inclusion from 1791 to 1828 in the Town of Halfmoon and Clifton Park's emergence from the same town. It thus symbolizes the close ties between the two towns, historically (the hamlet of Clifton Park is also partly in Halfmoon), and presently (commonality of major transportational routes, such as routes 9 and 146.

c) The bottom section of the shield includes the rolling land of Clifton Park along the Mohawk River. The stylized portrayal of the Mohawk River is representative of the Mohawk's transportational and agricultural importance to the growth and development of Clifton Park.

The ribbon with the date "1828" is wrapped about both external garlands and winds upward. It's placement within the seal not only reveals the date of Clifton Park's official status as a town, but also ties together the entire seal indicating unity and coherence, while its movement ending above the shield represents upwardness or continued growth and prosperity.

THREE PRESIDENTS CLAIM DUTCH HERITAGE

MARTIN VAN BUREN - 8TH President, of Kinderhook NY

THEODORE ROOSEVELT - 26TH President, of Oyster Bay NY

FRANKLIN D ROOSEVELT - 32ND President, of Hyde Park NY

ACKNOWLEDGEMENTS

CITY OF ALBANY - John Marsolais, City Clerk

CITY OF AMSTERDAM – Robert H. von Hasseln, City Historian

CITY OF HUDSON – Bonita Colwell, City Clerk, Alberta H Cox, Deputy Clerk
Columbia Board of Supvrs

CITY OF KINGSTON – Mayor James M. Sottile

CITY OF POUGHKEEPSIE – Deanne Flynn, City Chamberlain

CITY OF RENSSELAER – Mayor Dan Dwyer, Ernie Mann

CITY OF SCHENECTADY – Office of the Corporation Counsel

CITY OF TROY – Donna Ned, Sr. Planning Technician, Kathy Sheehan, RCHS

CITY OF WATERVLIET – Mayor Mike Manning, Historian Paul Murphy

NEW YORK CITY (MANHATTAN) – Mark Daly, Director of Communications
– Dept Citywide Admin

BOROUGH OF QUEENS - Roslyn Liturri, Press Office

TOWN OF BETHLEHEM – Kathleen Newkirk, Town Clerk

TOWN OF CATSKILL – Elizabeth C. Izzo, Town Clerk

TOWN OF CLAVERACK – Salvator Cozzolini, Town Historian

TOWN OF CLIFTON PARK – Pat O'Donnell, Town Clerk

TOWN OF COLONIE – Kevin Franklin, Town Historian

TOWN OF FISHKILL – Town Hall

TOWN OF GUILDERLAND – Alice Begley, Town Historian

TOWN OF HALF MOON – Mary Pearson, Town Clerk

TOWN OF HAVERSTRAW – Josephine Carella

TOWN OF HOOSICK – Susan Stradinger, Town Clerk

TOWN OF HYDE PARK – Carole Clearwater, Town Clerk, Pompey Delafield,
Town Supervisor

TOWN OF KINDERHOOK – Kim Pinkowski, Town Clerk

TOWN OF NEW SCOTLAND – Diane Deschenes, Town Clerk

TOWN OF NISKAYUNA –Helen Kopke, Town Clerk

TOWN OF NORTH GREENBUSH – Kathryn Connolly, Town Clerk

TOWN OF PITTSTOWN – Michelle Hoag, Town Clerk

TOWN OF RENSSELAERVILLE – Kathleen Hallenbeck, Town Clerk

TOWN OF RHINEBECK – Barb Cunningham, Town Clerk

TOWN OF ROTTERDAM – Eunice Esposito, Town Clerk

TOWN OF SCHAGHTICOKE – Janet Salisbury, Town Clerk, Jean Carlson Town Supervisor

TOWN OF SCHODACK – Diane L. Hutchinson, Schodack Town Historian

TOWN OF STEPHENTOWN – Beverly McClave, Stephentown Historical Society

TOWN OF STUYVESANT – Valerie Bertram, Town Supervisor, Melissa Naegeli, Town Clerk

ALBANY COUNTY – Jill Hughes, County Records, Hon Thomas G Clingan, County Clerk

COLUMBIA COUNTY – Holly C. Tanner, Columbia County Clerk, Mary Howell – Historian, Alex Cox Deputy Clerk, Board of Supervisors

GREENE COUNTY – Tracy Spitz, Admin Assistant, Carol Stevens, County Attorney

NASSAU COUNTY – Office of Tom Suozzi, County Executive

ORANGE COUNTY – Pat Weber, Orange County Historian's Office

RENSSELAER COUNTY (LEGISLATURE) – Jenet Marra, Clerk of the Legislature Christine Chesley, Director of Governmental Relations

ROCKLAND COUNTY - internet

SCHENECTADY COUNTY – Wendy Voelker, Special Events Coordinator

ULSTER COUNTY – Vincent C. Martello, Asst Deputy County Exec Communications

VILLAGE OF CATSKILL – Carolyn S. Pardy, Clerk, Treasurer

VILLAGE OF NASSAU – Margaret Van Deusen, Village Treasurer

VILLAGE OF SAUGERTIES – town website

VILLAGE OF TARRYTOWN – Carol Booth, Town Clerk, Richard Miller, Village Historian

VILLAGE OF SCOTIA – History of Glen Sanders Mansion

VILLAGE OF SLEEPY HOLLOW – Anthony P. Giaccio, Village Administrator

VILLAGE OF VALATIE – Village history by Dominick Lizzi, Village Historian